Divine Sync:

Maintaining a Strong Spiritual Connection with God

Divine Sync:

Maintaining a Strong Spiritual Connection with God

Dr. Tonya Williams

Acknowledgments

First and foremost, I would like to express my deepest gratitude to God, whose divine guidance and boundless love have been the cornerstone of this journey. Without His presence, this book would not have been possible.

To my family, your unwavering support and encouragement have been a constant source of strength and inspiration. Thank you for your patience, understanding, and belief in this vision. Your love has been a beacon of light throughout this process.

A heartfelt thank you to my friends and spiritual mentors, who have provided invaluable insights, wisdom, and prayers. Your words of encouragement and guidance have been instrumental in shaping the content and direction of this book.

To my editor, thank you for your meticulous attention to detail and commitment to bringing out the best in this manuscript. Your expertise and dedication have helped refine and polish the ideas presented here.

A special thanks to my church, *Releasing Living Waters Ministries,* whose support and prayers have enriched my understanding of divine connection and spiritual growth. Your faith and dedication have truly inspired me.

I am also deeply grateful to my readers. Your hunger for spiritual growth and connection with God fuels my passion to write and share these insights. May this book serve as a guide and companion on your journey of Divine Sync.

Finally, to everyone who has supported this endeavor in large and small ways, your contributions have not gone unnoticed. Thank you for believing in this book's message and helping to bring it to life.

With sincere gratitude,

Dr. Tonya Williams

Table of Contents

Introduction

Unleashing the Power of Divine Sync

Welcome to the extraordinary journey of "Divine Sync: Maintaining a Strong Spiritual Connection with God." As I reflect on this book's profound insights and revelations, I am filled with a sense of awe and wonder at the depths of wisdom that await you.

In this fast-paced digital age, we are familiar with syncing our devices to Wi-Fi. We understand the importance of staying connected and ensuring that our data from multiple devices is transferred seamlessly. But what if I told you that a higher level of syncing is available to us—a spiritual connection that transcends the limitations of technology?

In these pages, you will discover the power of "Divine Sync"—the ability to connect with the heart of God, receive divine downloads, and align yourself with His purposes. Just as syncing to the cloud allows us to access and share information effortlessly, our relationship with the Lord enables us to tap into the divine realm and receive supernatural insight and direction.

To further help you process Divine Sync, *Connection Keys: Sync Glossary of Terms* has been added to guide your deep dive into this connection with God.

As you embark on this transformative adventure, may the harmony of revelation and strategy resonate throughout your journey. May you experience the joy and fulfillment of aligning yourself with God's purposes and walking in sync with the Lord.

Get ready to unleash the power of divine sync and embark on a journey that will forever transform your relationship with God and your understanding of His purposes.

The journey starts now!

Chapter 1

The Divine Network:
Exploring the Concept of Syncing to God's Presence

As we embark on this journey together, I am excited to explore the concept of the Divine Network and its significance in our lives. In today's digitally interconnected world, we expect to be able to connect and sync any number of electronic gadgets—including our cell phones, tablets, and computers—to the internet, effortlessly accessing information and communicating with others. But beneath all human innovations and technologies lies an even more powerful network. This connection is known as the Divine Network—the network of God's presence and guidance in our lives.

Recognizing God's omnipresence is the first step toward comprehending the Divine Network. Time and space do not confine Him to a physical location. Rather, His presence permeates every aspect of creation. God's presence envelops us, ready for access and experience, just as the airwaves carry signals around us.

Being in harmony with God's will is not some abstract idea; it can and will change our lives. It's as essential that our lives sync with God's plans as the devices we use sync with a network.

We must learn of His presence and draw closer to Him. The awareness of God's constant nearness compels us to walk closer to Him. Only when we are close to the Wi-Fi signal source can we strengthen our connection to a Wi-Fi network. Similarly, prayer, worship, and seeking His presence strengthen our link with the Creator of all networks. These bring us closer to God. It allows us to tap into His heavenly network.

Connecting to God's Wi-Fi through prayer is like gaining access to God's presence, surrendering our hearts and desires to Him, and aligning ourselves with His will. There are different forms of prayer, such as intercession, supplication, and thanksgiving, as well as ways to enhance our connection to the divine network.

We gain entrance into God's presence through our worship. Worship, like Wi-Fi, requires a connection to a network to access the Internet; it is how we communicate with the Lord. Worship is a powerful means of strengthening our connection to the Lord. Through worship, we position our hearts to encounter God's presence, inviting Him to move and speak in our lives. Worship transforms us; it shifts our

focus from ourselves to God and strengthens our bond with the Lord.

We can fortify our relationship with His heavenly network by growing closer to God. Drawing from David's intimate relationship with God (Psalm 63:1–8), the power of spending time in His presence, studying His Word, and developing a personal relationship with Him only deepens our intimacy and enhances our access to His divine network.

Being in sync with God brings an array of benefits. It allows us to experience His peace that surpasses all understanding, even amid chaos and uncertainty. It opens the door to divine guidance, enabling us to navigate the complexities of life with wisdom and discernment. Moreover, syncing with God's presence invites supernatural provision into our lives as we trust His abundant provision and faithfulness. The Word of God, via Matthew 6:33, says, "But seek ye first the kingdom of God and His righteousness; and all these things shall be added unto you."

Cultivating a lifestyle of syncing with God's presence requires intentional effort and commitment. We must develop practical strategies to build this deep connection. Just as a close relationship requires time, effort, and vulnerability, our relationship with God thrives when we invest in it. Immersing ourselves in His Word is a strategy to create a spiritual atmosphere that fosters a deep connection with God and allows us to sync with His divine network.

We must overcome obstacles if we are ever to tune in fully to God's presence. The cares of the world, the busyness of life, and the noise surrounding us can all disrupt our connection with God. We must learn how to overcome these barriers by creating intentional moments of connection, eliminating distractions, and carving out sacred space for God.

Let's accept and embrace God's omnipresence and recognize that we can connect with Him in every moment, whether in times of happiness and joy or sorrow and pain. Our divine connection encompasses every aspect of our lives. When we remain in His presence, we will always walk in His plan and purpose for our lives. Furthermore, we will consistently maintain our connection to the Divine Network and align with His presence.

In conclusion, this chapter has laid the groundwork for comprehending the Divine Network and its profound implications. We have explored the importance of connecting to God's presence, understanding His omnipresence, and syncing our lives with His divine plan. The benefits of being in sync with God are immeasurable—His peace, guidance, and supernatural provision are available to us.

As we continue through this book, I hope you'll go deeper in your spiritual walk with Him to align with God's presence and discover the life-altering effects of the Divine Network for yourself.

Chapter 2

Signal Strength:
Building Your Connection to the Lord

Like a stable Wi-Fi signal that ensures uninterrupted data transfer, we must strengthen our connection with God. A strong relationship with God allows us to sense His presence, receive divine insights, and align with His will. We must learn to be more in tune with our spiritual selves to deepen our relationship with God. We must tune into God's frequency to hear His voice and see His hand at work. This level of sensitivity involves cultivating a deep relationship with Him, practicing stillness, and listening attentively to the promptings of the Holy Spirit.

Our faith in God should serve as the cornerstone of every relationship. It is not merely about surface-level encounters; it's about developing a deep, genuine connection with the One who made everything. James 4:8 states, "Draw nigh to God, and He will draw nigh to you," emphasizing the need to actively pursue God and come near Him. It flourishes when we make strengthening our connection with Him a top priority.

Prayer serves as a powerful tool for strengthening our connection to the Lord. It is how we communicate with God: pouring out our hearts, seeking His guidance, and aligning our desires with His. Jesus, for example, shows us the importance of maintaining an active and continuous prayer life by demonstrating the power of a close relationship with God.

Fasting and prayer - Combining the two further strengthens the signal. By consistently praying and fasting while seeking God's face and aligning our hearts with His, we become more receptive to God's guidance and wisdom.

Strengthening our connection to the Lord involves deepening our knowledge of God's Word. We must study and meditate on Scripture, allowing it to shape our thinking and align us with God's heart. The Word of God is a foundation for discernment, providing wisdom and guidance for our daily lives. The Holy Spirit speaks to and through us through the Word of God. He puts words in our mouths to say things we don't know on our own. He provides direction during spiritual and literal wilderness experiences. His Word denotes His presence. So, the stronger our depth of study and submission to His Word, the better our connection to Him will be.

Cultivating a worship lifestyle is another critical aspect of strengthening our connection to the Lord. Worship is not only something we do on Sundays. It's more than singing slow songs and lifting one's hand in adoration. It's an attitude of giving God the glory He deserves in all we do. As we engage in heartfelt worship through singing, praising God, meditating on the Word, or submitting our talents and gifts to Him, we make room for His presence and strengthen our connection.

Just as a strong Wi-Fi signal requires eliminating interference, we must remove distractions that hinder our connection with God. The world's influences and negative thought patterns can constantly interrupt our lives. Environmental circumstances can degrade our connection with God.

It takes work and purposefulness to keep a strong connection with God. Spiritual barriers disrupt our communion with God. To achieve our goals, we need the ability to concentrate, free our minds of distractions, and set aside time for God. Deliberately making room for God and clearing the clutter from our lives improves our ability to hear His voice.

In the same way, multiple devices can connect to the same Wi-Fi network, so we must strive to support one another. We can strengthen one another on our spiritual path and delight in God's presence through fellowship, accountability, and corporate worship. Being part of a church reinforces our connection to the Lord. Surrounding ourselves with like-

minded believers can encourage, challenge, and support us in our spiritual journey. Being part of a group allows us to bounce ideas off one another, pick up new information, and pray for direction from God as a group.

Strengthening our connection to the Lord is a continuous process of seeking, listening, and aligning ourselves with God's heart and purposes. We can experience a deep connection to the Lord by developing spiritual sensitivity, removing distractions, praying and fasting, deepening our knowledge of God's Word, cultivating a lifestyle of worship, seeking a godly community, and cultivating humility and obedience. This will allow the anointing to flow with greater clarity and power.

Chapter 3

Establishing a Stable Connection: Building a Strong Relationship with God

Intercessors must realize that a strong connection with God is the foundation for connecting to the Divine Network. Just as a reliable connection is necessary for effective communication, so is a close relationship with God to feel His love and benefit from His wisdom. Establishing a solid and lasting bond with God requires an intentional pursuit of intimacy.

There are people in the Bible who had a strong relationship with God. Abraham, the father of faith, had an unshakeable relationship with God. From his example of obedient trust in the Lord, we learn about the life-altering effects of developing a close relationship with God.

Moses, chosen to lead the Israelites out of Egypt, exhibited an intimate friendship with God. Through his experiences at the burning bush and ongoing conversations with the Lord, we witness the importance of open and honest communication in fostering a strong connection. Moses's willingness to listen and respond to God's instructions deepened their relationship and led to remarkable acts of deliverance.

David, the beloved king and psalmist, provides a powerful example of authentic worship and a heart set on seeking God. We witness David's vulnerability, transparency, and unwavering trust in God through the Psalms. From the example of David, we see that cultivating a heart of worship, even amid trials and triumphs, strengthens our connection with the Lord and aligns us with His purposes.

When we pray, we open a channel of communication with God in which we can share our most intimate feelings, hopes, and requests with Him. Worship and prayer become powerful vehicles for establishing a stable connection with God. By entering His presence with reverence, adoration, and thanksgiving, we create an atmosphere where our hearts align with His. The more we invest in our relationships, the more God can make His presence felt in our daily lives. Developing a strong connection with God is a life-altering and gratifying endeavor.

A stable connection with God is essential for connecting to the Divine Network. The stories of Abraham, Moses, and David teach us valuable lessons about the impact of prayer, worship, and seeking God's closeness.

As we face the various trials that will inevitably come our way, let us work diligently to strengthen the bond with the Lord, secure in the knowledge that only through a solid and lasting commitment to Him may we enter His presence and live the entire fruitful life He has in store for us.

Auto-Sync Mode:
Cultivating and Stabilizing a Lifestyle of Spiritual Sensitivity

Just as our devices can always remain connected to Wi-Fi when we're in the presence of the modem, we can experience a continuous sync with the Lord, walking in His presence and receiving His ongoing guidance and revelation.

Maintaining a close and personal relationship with God throughout the day means living in constant communion with Him. It's about making a habit of always being alert to God's presence and receptive to His guidance.

We need to develop a heightened awareness of God's presence to walk in constant communion. We must cultivate this awareness by practicing mindfulness, regularly pausing to acknowledge God's presence, and inviting Him into every moment of our day. By cultivating a lifestyle of awareness, we create space for God to speak, guide, and reveal Himself to us in ways we might have never imagined.

Living in constant communion with God requires us to develop a responsive heart that is sensitive to His leading and prompted to obey His voice. Cultivating a heart of obedience, surrender, and humility allows God to shape and mold us according to His will. By developing a responsive heart, we align ourselves with God's purposes, creating a space where we can hear His voice and follow His guidance.

When we walk in constant communion with God, we enter into a divine flow where His thoughts become our thoughts, and His desires become our desires. There is beauty in surrendering to this flow and trusting in God's perfect plan and timing. Relinquishing control and allowing God to guide us on a remarkable journey of purpose and fulfillment brings us freedom and joy.

Continuously syncing with God necessitates an ongoing posture of surrender and submission. We must surrender our wills, desires, and plans to God, aligning ourselves with His purposes. We must submit our lives to His Lordship daily and seek His will in all decisions. Surrender and submission create an atmosphere of openness to His guidance and willingness to follow His lead.

Walking in constant communion with God involves seeking divine alignment in every area of our lives. We must align our thoughts, attitudes, and actions with God's Word and character. This alignment ensures that we are in sync with His heart and purposes, enabling us to walk in obedience and experience the fullness of His presence and power.

Learning to listen to God daily is essential for staying in constant sync and having a stable connection with Him. We must still have our thoughts and emotions to hear God speak to us. God speaks to us through His Word, the Holy Spirit,

wise advice, and even our circumstances. It is through these means we have a stable connection and flow in Him. Walking in constant communion allows us to have a stable connection with Him and keep us auto synced to what He wants whenever he wants it.

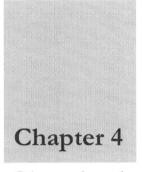

Chapter 4

Discerning the Times:
Understanding God's Will in a Changing World

We live in an era where the landscape of society, culture, and technology constantly evolves, presenting new challenges and opportunities. To thrive in this dynamic world, we need to hone our powers of discernment and stay in step with God's plans.

Understanding the relevance of knowing the times requires looking at Jesus' words. Jesus rebukes the Pharisees and Sadducees in Matthew 16:3b (NIV). He said: "You know how to interpret the appearance of the sky, but you cannot interpret the signs of the times." Jesus emphasized the importance of perceiving the spiritual climate and understanding the deeper meaning behind current events. Similarly, in Luke 12:54–56, He invites the crowd to discern the signs of the weather and applies the same principle to recognize the signs of the times.

The Holy Spirit, our precious gift as believers, guides us into all truth and helps us comprehend God's deeper purposes. With the Spirit's help, we can better grasp the times in which we live and adjust our priorities to fit with God's will.

We must equip ourselves with practical tools and strategies for discerning the signs of the times. We must give ourselves to listening to Him. Listening to the still, small voice of the Holy Spirit, allows Him to be a lamp to our feet and a light to our path (Psalm 119:105). Also, we must immerse ourselves in the Scriptures. In His Word, we gain insight into God's character, His redemptive plan, and the principles that govern His kingdom. Lastly, prayer and seeking Him helps us to discern His will in a changing world. These tools, when used correctly, allows us to discern the times.

The Bible provides us with examples of people who had outstanding insight. By interpreting Pharaoh's dreams, Joseph could foresee the coming famine and help Egypt prepare for it. We learn from Daniel that we can pray for insight and rely on God's revelation to understand the times we live in. These scriptural examples are perpetual reminders of the importance of using our discernment to follow God's will.

Cultivating a listening ear to the Holy Spirit, understanding who God is through the word of God, and praying and seeking Him are all essential to discerning the times. In a world filled with noise and distractions, creating moments of silence and solitude allows the Spirit to speak to our hearts and provide divine guidance. Further, the times of study we previously had will then translate during our quiet times, when revelation is revealed. All of this will allow us to discern the times by way of the Holy Spirit.

As a bonus, and as previously stated, we mustn't be afraid to seek guidance from trusted spiritual mentors and be part of active Christian communities that encourage and support shared understanding and insight. The bonus of a community only allows the community to confirm what each has received individually and give further insight to others who may need clarity, encouragement, or understanding.

Discerning the times can only occur when we're in Divine Sync. If we're not synced, understanding God's will cannot happen.

Chapter 5

Navigating Divine Downloads:
Receiving and Applying God's Revelations

Just as a computer receives and processes data, we, as believers, receive divine downloads from our Heavenly Father. These revelations (downloads) are gifts of wisdom, guidance, and understanding that equip us to navigate the complexities of life with divine insight.

Before understanding aspects of receiving and applying God's revelations, it is essential to grasp the nature of these divine downloads.

Rather than being the product of human reasoning, God has revealed revelations to us. God, in His role as Creator, possesses boundless wisdom and insight, which He generously shares to enable us to align with His perfect will.

There are various channels through which God communicates His revelations to us. Just as there are different ways to transfer data, God uses multiple avenues to speak to our hearts and minds. We examine the power of His

Word, the Bible, the primary source of divine revelation. We will also investigate the role of prayer, worship, dreams, visions, and the inner witness of the Holy Spirit in receiving God's messages. Understanding these channels helps us to recognize and discern the divine downloads we receive.

Just like a digital download transfers essential data to our devices, divine downloads carry profound wisdom, direction, and guidance for our lives. They are like treasure chests filled with heavenly treasures waiting for discovery.

We learn in the Bible that both Moses and the prophets received revelations from God, such as the Ten Commandments at Mount Sinai or instructions on preparing for war. These divine encounters altered their lives and ultimately influenced history. We, as Christians, need to know how divine downloads work. It enables us to understand, absorb, and practice these heavenly revelations daily. It gives us the strength to do what God wants so we live the full, abundant lives He has planned for us.

Developing a Listening Ear

Efficiently receiving and acting upon divine insights requires developing a keen listening ear. To have a good spiritual connection, we need to be humble and listen to God's voice, just as we need to pay attention to signals for a good internet connection. We must train our ears to listen by spending time alone, reading, reflecting on God's Word, and being quiet. Hearing and discerning God's voice is paramount in divine downloads. Just as a radio needs a precise frequency to receive signals, we must tune our hearts and minds to the frequency of God's voice.

Developing a listening ear entails creating an atmosphere of stillness and attentiveness in which we intentionally position ourselves to hear from God. It requires us to quiet the noise of the world around us and cultivate a spirit of humility and receptivity. Just as the prophet Samuel learned to say, "Speak Lord, for your servant is listening" (1 Samuel 3:10; AMPC), we too must adopt a posture of surrender and readiness to receive. Spending time praying, meditating on God's Word, and cultivating a heart of worship are critical components of developing a sensitive spirit to God's voice.

Applying Divine Revelations

Receiving divine downloads is the beginning; true transformation occurs when we apply these revelations. Obedience and faithfulness are essential to acting upon God's instructions. When we align our actions with His revealed truth, we experience the fullness of His blessings and witness the fulfillment of His purposes in and through us.

Applying divine revelations involves taking the insights and wisdom we receive from God and integrating them into our thoughts, words, and actions. It necessitates aligning our lives with the revealed truth and guidance, making intentional choices that reflect the divine downloads we have received.

Let's begin with the Apostle Paul's obedience to the revelation he received on the road to Damascus. The story of the Apostle Paul's encounter with Jesus on the road to Damascus is a powerful example of applying divine revelations to our lives. Paul, previously known as Saul, persecuted Christians until he had a life-changing encounter with Jesus Christ. This encounter revealed who Jesus was and how it transformed Paul's life and mission.

One practical way to apply divine revelations inspired by Paul's obedience is to be willing to surrender and submit to the leading of the Holy Spirit. Paul didn't resist or ignore the revelation he received on the road to Damascus; instead, he humbly accepted it and allowed it to redirect the course of his life. Similarly, when we receive divine revelations, we must be willing to submit our plans, desires, and ambitions to God's will, trusting that His plans are higher and more significant than our own.

Another practical way to apply divine revelations is to seek confirmation and wise counsel. After his encounter with Jesus, Paul sought confirmation from Ananias, a disciple of Jesus, who affirmed the validity of the revelation and baptized him. Seeking wise counsel from trusted spiritual mentors and leaders can help us gain further clarity and guidance in applying the divine revelations we receive. Their insights and perspectives can provide valuable advice and ensure we align our actions with God's will.

Furthermore, Paul's obedience to the revelation led to a radical transformation in his character and lifestyle. He went from persecuting Christians to becoming one of the greatest champions of the Gospel. This change reminds us that applying divine revelations involves making internal shifts and practical changes in our attitudes, behaviors, and actions. It requires us to let go of old patterns, embrace new ways of thinking, and actively live out the truth and values revealed.

Applying divine revelations involves:

- Surrendering to the leading of the Holy Spirit.

- Seeking confirmation and wise counsel.

- Making practical changes in our lives to align with the truth revealed to us.

Drawing inspiration from the Apostle Paul's obedience on the road to Damascus, we can cultivate a heart of humility, seek guidance from trusted mentors, and allow divine revelations to transform our character and actions. In doing so, we open ourselves to experiencing the fullness of God's purposes and walking in alignment with His will.

Yielding to the Holy Spirit's Work

The Holy Spirit's primary role in automatic updates is to impact our spiritual lives. Drawing from passages such as John 16:13, "Howbeit when He, the Spirit of Truth, is come, He will guide you into all truth: for He shall not speak of Himself; but whatsoever He shall hear, that shall He speak;

and He will show you things to come," we explore how the Holy Spirit guides us, convicts us, and empowers us to embrace the updates that God desires to bring about. We must surrender and cooperate with the Holy Spirit's work, allowing Him to renew and transform us from the inside out.

Yielding to the work of the Holy Spirit is crucial to navigating divine downloads and applying God's revelations. The Holy Spirit is the revealer of truth and the transformative agent in our lives. Just as a sculptor molds clay into a beautiful masterpiece, the Holy Spirit desires to shape and mold us into the likeness of Christ.

To yield to the Holy Spirit's work, we must cultivate a posture of surrender and openness. By surrendering our plans, desires, and agendas, we allow the Holy Spirit full access to our hearts and minds. This surrender means relinquishing control and humbly submitting ourselves to His leading and guidance. As we yield to the Holy Spirit's work, He empowers us to walk in alignment with God's will and enables us to live out the divine revelations we receive.

Additionally, yielding to the Holy Spirit's work requires humility and teachability. It recognizes that we don't have all the answers and need the Holy Spirit's wisdom and guidance to navigate the complexities of life. We must be receptive to correction, allow the Holy Spirit to challenge our perspectives, and be willing to learn and grow our understanding of God's truth.

Moreover, yielding to the Holy Spirit's work involves active participation. It is not a passive surrender but an intentional cooperation with the Spirit's transformative work in our lives. This active participation may include embracing spiritual disciplines such as prayer, meditation on the Scriptures, and fellowship with other believers. It may require stepping out in faith, embracing new opportunities, and embracing the uncomfortable process of growth and change.

As we yield to the Holy Spirit's work, we can experience God's transformative power in our lives. The Lord will soften our hearts, renew our minds, and align our actions with God's purposes. We become vessels through which God's love, grace, and power flow. Yielding to the Holy Spirit's work enables us to walk in the fullness of our divine destiny and effectively witness God's kingdom.

Yielding to the Holy Spirit's work is essential to navigating divine downloads and applying God's revelations. By surrendering, cultivating humility, and actively participating in the Spirit's transformative work, we open ourselves up to a life of alignment with God's will and experience the power of His transformation in every area of our lives.

Be Open to God's Grace

As we open ourselves to God's grace, He performs automatic updates. As software updates bring about improvements and fixes, God's grace works to heal, restore, and refine us.

Drawing inspiration from 2 Corinthians 12:9, "And He said unto me, My grace is sufficient for thee; for my strength is made perfect in weakness. Therefore I will most gladly glory in my infirmities, that the power of Christ may rest upon me." God's grace enables us to let go of our shortcomings and receive His transformational power.

We must open ourselves to God's grace in navigating divine downloads and applying God's revelations. Grace is God's unmerited favor and His empowering presence in our lives. A flower opens its petals to receive sunlight and rain, calling us to open ourselves to God's abundant grace. Opening ourselves to God's grace starts with recognizing our need for Him. It acknowledges that we are imperfect and fall short of God's perfect standard. We understand that we cannot earn or deserve His favor, but He freely gives it to us through the finished work of Jesus Christ on the cross.

By opening ourselves to God's grace, we release the burden of trying to earn His approval and embrace His unconditional love and acceptance. Through His grace, we are empowered to receive and apply His revelations. His grace forgives, transforms, and equips us to walk in obedience and righteousness.

To open ourselves to God's grace, we must relinquish self-reliance and surrender to His love and mercy. We come to Him humbly, acknowledging our need for His guidance, strength, and wisdom. We trust in His faithfulness and rely on His promises to sustain us.

Moreover, opening ourselves to God's grace means embracing a posture of surrender and dependency. It recognizes that apart from Him, we can do nothing, but all things are possible with Him. We yield our will and desires to His perfect will, trusting that His plans for us are good and His ways are higher than our own.

As we open ourselves to God's grace, we experience the transformative power of His love in our lives. His grace empowers us to walk in obedience, overcome challenges, and fulfill our divine purpose. We become vessels of His grace, extending it to others and participating in His redemptive work.

Opening ourselves to God's grace is vital to navigating divine downloads and applying God's revelations. Recognizing our need for Him, surrendering to His love, and embracing His unmerited favor, we position ourselves to receive His guidance, strength, and wisdom. Let us open our hearts and lives to God's abundant grace and experience the fullness of His transformative power on our faith journey.

Cultivating a Teachable Spirit

Over my life, I've learned to cultivate a teachable spirit and allow God to renew and transform me. He can do the same for you.

Drawing from passages like Proverbs 9:9, "Give instruction to a wise man, and he will be yet wiser; teach a just man, and he will increase in learning," we explore the transformative power of humility, openness, and a willingness to learn. Being teachable allows us to receive God's updates with a receptive heart, embracing His wisdom and guidance.

Cultivating a teachable spirit is paramount to navigating divine downloads and applying God's revelations. It is about embracing humility and having the attitude of learning from God. Just as students eagerly listen to their teacher and remain open to new knowledge, we are called to approach God with a teachable spirit.

Cultivating a teachable spirit begins with recognizing that we have much to learn from our heavenly Father. It acknowledges that His wisdom surpasses our own and that His ways are higher than ours. It means humbling ourselves before Him and surrendering our preconceived notions, biases, and limited understanding.

As we cultivate a teachable spirit, we become open to the Holy Spirit's guidance and correction. We invite God to speak into our lives, challenge our perspectives, and refine our character. We are willing to allow God's loving hands to mold us because we understand that our faith journey is a lifelong process of growth and transformation.

A thirst for knowledge and a willingness to align our lives with God's Word are characteristics of a teachable spirit. It eagerly seeks His guidance through prayer and studying His Scriptures, allowing His truth to shape our thoughts, attitudes, and actions. It is being open to the Holy Spirit's conviction and correction, knowing that His guidance leads us to a deeper understanding of God's will.

Moreover, cultivating a teachable spirit involves embracing the value of learning from others. The willingness to receive wisdom and insights from fellow believers, mentors, and spiritual leaders can help us grow in our understanding of God's revelations. It recognizes that we are part of a larger body of Christ, where each member has a unique contribution.

Cultivating a teachable spirit is essential to navigating divine downloads and applying God's revelations. We grow in wisdom and understanding by embracing humility, seeking God's guidance, and learning from His Word and others. Let's approach God with a humble and receptive heart, ready to learn from His wisdom and experience His truth.

Chapter 6

Accelerating the Divine Download

As fast internet connectivity allows for quick data transfers, we explore practical ways to accelerate the reception of divine downloads and insights. Cultivating a listening posture, embracing humility, and creating space for God to speak can speed up receiving divine revelations.

The Need for Accelerated Revelation

When we receive timely and accurate divine downloads, they can equip us to navigate challenges, make wise decisions, and fulfill God's purposes. Just as fast internet speeds enhance productivity and efficiency, accelerated revelation empowers us to walk in step with God's plans and experience greater, more significant spiritual growth.

Cultivating a Posture of Listening

We must develop a posture of listening to receive divine downloads at a faster pace. Imagine yourself as a vessel ready to catch every drop of wisdom from the Lord. Your

spiritual posture determines how swiftly you receive insights and revelations. The key is to have a listening posture—a state of receptivity that positions you to hear His whispers.

In 1 Samuel 3:10 and 1 Kings 19:12, Samuel and Elijah model the art of positioning themselves to hear God's voice. Samuel, in the stillness of the night, responded, "Speak, for thy servant heareth." His posture of openness and readiness enabled him to receive divine instruction. Elijah, amid a tumultuous experience, encountered God's voice in a gentle whisper. His story highlights the importance of listening in moments of stillness. Samuel and Elijah demonstrate how a quiet heart can be a gateway to divine insights.

Picture your heart as a sanctuary of stillness where God's voice can echo clearly. Cultivating this environment involves intentional practices. Accept solitude as a sacred retreat from the noise of life. Prioritize moments of quiet reflection, allowing your mind to settle and your spirit to open.

Embracing Humility

Humility is a critical factor in accelerating the reception of divine downloads. Pride can hinder the flow of revelation, while humility can open us up to receiving from God.

Drawing inspiration from passages such as James 4:6 and Proverbs 11:2, the transformative power of humility in our relationship with God can be noted. By acknowledging our dependence on Him and recognizing His wisdom, we create a space for accelerated revelation.

Creating Space for God to Speak

Similar to creating bandwidth for faster internet speeds, creating space for God to speak means setting aside dedicated time for prayer and meditation, engaging in regular fasting, and intentionally removing distractions that hinder our ability to hear from God. We readily open ourselves to receiving divine downloads by prioritizing and protecting this sacred space.

Developing a Hunger for Revelation

Developing a hunger for divine revelation is a catalyst for accelerated downloads and cultivating a thirst for God's wisdom and insights, which fuels our desire to seek Him more fervently. Drawing from passages like Psalm 42:1-2 and Matthew 5:6, we explore the power of hungering and thirsting for righteousness and how it propels us towards accelerated revelation.

Praying for Divine Downloads

Just like we can send a request for information through the internet, intentional and fervent prayer can facilitate the flow of revelation. Prayer strategies include:

- Asking God for specific insights.

- Praying in alignment with His Word.

- Seeking the Holy Spirit's guidance.

By engaging in consistent and focused prayer, we open ourselves to receiving divine downloads more swiftly.

Applying and Acting on Revelation

Applying and acting on the divine downloads we receive from God and promptly obeying His instructions demonstrates our faith and paves the way for further divine downloads. By stepping out in obedience, we position ourselves to receive ongoing revelations and experience an acceleration of divine downloads in our lives.

Chapter 7

Seamless Integration: Aligning with God's Plan

Just as modern devices seamlessly connect with the cloud to access and share data effortlessly, this chapter delves into the profound concept of aligning our lives to receive data related to God's divine plan. It emphasizes the transformative **power of surrender, trust, and obedience,** which helps us align to receive and align with God's divine plan.

The Call to Surrender

Devices need to connect and sync with the cloud to receive codes and software updates. The same is true of our lives. We must yield ourselves to God's guidance and surrender our will to Him.

To elaborate on the call to surrender, consider the passages of Proverbs 3:5–6 and Jeremiah 29:11. They highlight the importance of trusting God's plan and surrendering to His leading.

As we navigate surrendering to the divine plan—a concept as essential to our spiritual journey as syncing is to technology, imagine your life as a device seeking optimal functionality through a connection to the cloud. By aligning your will with God's plan, you can ensure a harmonious collaboration between your desires and divine design, resulting in your best functionality.

The Art of Surrender

Let's understand the intricate art of surrender, underscoring its significance in your spiritual journey. Just as technology thrives when synced with the cloud, your life flourishes when aligned with God's will. It's akin to plugging into the divine "cloud," where you relinquish your plans and sync your heart with His intentions.

Yielding to the Master's plan means surrendering your plans and desires and letting His plan become your plan. Embrace surrendering your plans and desires and letting His plan become your plan. It involves releasing control and acknowledging that God's plan surpasses your understanding. Let's remember Jesus in the Garden of Gethsemane (Luke 22:42), where He prayed, "Not my will but Yours be done." This momentous surrender is a blueprint for syncing your will with the divine plan.

Surrender and Transformation

When devices and the cloud are in seamless harmony, updates or changes can occur quickly on devices. Your life transformation will quickly happen as you surrender to God's plan.

Surrender is not a sign of weakness but an act of strength, allowing God's transformative power to work in you. Paul's transformation from a persecutor of Christians to an apostle of Christ showcases how surrender can lead to profound change.

Syncing for Harmony

Reflect on the harmony achieved when devices sync seamlessly with the cloud. Likewise, surrendering your will to God's plan creates a harmonious alignment with His purposes. Surrender involves releasing control and acknowledging that God's plan surpasses your understanding. This alignment brings peace, purpose, and life in sync with the divine.

The Trust Factor

Trust forms the cornerstone of this surrender process. Just as devices trust the cloud's security to store their data, you must trust God's wisdom and goodness to shape your life's trajectory. Proverbs 3:5–6 echoes this sentiment, encouraging you to "trust in the Lord with all your heart and lean not on your own understanding." Further, we must trust God's sovereignty and believe His plan is perfect and for our ultimate good. The passages of Psalm 37:5 and Isaiah 55:8–9 remind us of God's faithfulness and higher ways.

Divine Design Unveiled

Consider Jeremiah 29:11 a beacon of hope in times of uncertainty. "For I know the plans I have for you," declares the Lord, "plans to prosper you and not to harm you, plans to give you hope and a future." This scripture unveils God's divine design, assuring you that His plans are always for your ultimate good. Just as devices achieve optimal performance by syncing with the right cloud, your life achieves purpose and fulfillment through God's perfect plan, which we must trust and embrace.

Obedience and Alignment

Let us explore the significance of obedience in aligning ourselves with God's plan. Just as devices must follow the prescribed protocols to integrate with the cloud seamlessly, we discuss the importance of obeying God's Word by drawing insights from passages such as John 14:23 and Romans 12:2. These verses emphasize the power of obedience, which supports our alignment to divine sync.

Walking in Step with the Spirit

The capacity to receive real-time information is guided by the Holy Spirit. If we walk in the Spirit, as stated by passages such as Galatians 5:25 and Romans 8:14, which highlight the transformative power of walking in step with the Spirit, we will remain sensitive to God's plan. He will prompt us, and

we will need to follow Him. Walking in the Spirit further promotes seamless synchronization with Him.

Our obedience to walk in step with the Spirit will improve alignment. If we dilly-dally in our trust, there is a lack of obedience. This action will clog our connection to Him and move us out of alignment. It will impact our peace and clarity and deter us from divine sync.

An Invitation to Sync

As technology beckons you to synchronize your data for optimal performance, the Lord extends an invitation to sync your will with God's plan. Surrender is not about forfeiting your desires but about aligning them with the higher purpose God has for you. Just as you enjoy the benefits of cloud-synced devices, surrender offers the benefits of a life synchronized with the divine flow.

Obedience causes us to walk in step with His spirit. It means that when He sends a message, we respond to it. We do what He says to do, and we speak whatever He says we ought to speak. Obedience helps us continue to walk seamlessly in alignment with His plan.

When we align with God's plan, we recognize the beauty and significance of living in sync with His divine purposes. By surrendering to Him, trusting in His sovereignty, obeying His commands, seeking divine guidance, and walking in step with the Holy Spirit, we can experience the seamless integration of our lives with God's plan. Aligning ourselves

with God's plan brings fulfillment, purpose, and a life that bears fruit for His glory. Be inspired to align with God's plan, knowing true joy and abundant life in His perfect design is available.

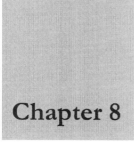

Chapter 8

Guarding Against Spiritual Attacks: Strengthening Your Divine Sync Security

Security is vital in the realm of divine sync. Just as networks are safeguarded against threats, your connection with God requires vigilant protection.

As we delve into this chapter, let's explore how to shield our spiritual connection from malevolent disruptions.

Defending Your Divine Network

Imagine our spiritual sync as a network with priceless data flowing between us and the Lord. It needs to be protected and have a defense mechanism.

Just as 1 Peter 5:8 warns of a lurking adversary seeking to disrupt the priceless data flow between us and the Lord, so does our journey echo the story of Job. His life, a battlefield of trials, is a testament to the power of steadfast faith amidst adversity. Despite facing the storm, Job's unyielding trust in God was an impenetrable firewall. Job's story exemplifies

how steadfast faith and the armor of God's truth can guard against spiritual breaches.

Advanced security systems protect networks and establish a spiritual firewall to prevent interruptions. We can create a spiritual firewall through prayer, reading the Scriptures, and discernment. Building our spiritual firewall—the combination of prayer, reading the Word, and discernment—will become a source code to keep a firewall between us and the disrupter.

We should regularly sync with the divine source code. We should recognize that the enemy seeks out vulnerabilities, which requires building a spiritual firewall.

Detecting the Trojan Horses

Beware of Trojan horses—malware that disguises itself as legitimate code or software. Spiritually, Trojan horses are subtle temptations that can breach your sync. They come in the form of doubt, fear, and compromise. Reflect on Joseph's wisdom, who fled from temptation, and allow it to mirror your response. Recognize these insidious threats and confront them with the sword of God's Word. Just as Joseph fled Potiphar's wife's advances, you too can detect and defeat Trojan horses. Your divine sync depends on your ability to recognize these lurking threats and thwart them with God's Word.

Responding to Data Breaches

A data breach disrupts or compromises an individual's spiritual connection with God. This breach can be caused by external spiritual attacks, internal vulnerabilities such as doubt or fear, or distractions that weaken faith and alignment with God's will. Similar to how unauthorized access or malicious activities compromise a digital network, a spiritual data breach signifies the intrusion of negative influences that disrupt the flow of divine wisdom, guidance, and protection in one's life.

When a breach occurs, we cannot panic. Like Job, we must allow resilience and faith in God to rebuild our sync. Understand that challenges are not failures but rather stepping stones for growth. Remember, every breach can be repaired, and every stolen fragment of our spiritual data can be restored. View these moments as divine system checks, realigning your synchronicity with God's greater purpose.

Responding to a data breach involves recognizing the disruption, reinforcing our faith, and taking corrective measures to restore and strengthen the spiritual connection with God.

Upgrading Your Spiritual Security

As devices require regular software security updates, so does our spiritual protection, which demands consistent enhancements. Remain in sync with the Holy Spirit, using His guidance to detect lurking threats. An untitled heart or a

past failure that's remembered today requires a spiritual upgrade in our security. The higher we align with Him, the more He will reveal what He wants to change in us. We must seek divine guidance as diligently as we would the latest security patch. Spiritual security upgrades will always function as we equip ourselves with faith, prayer, and fellow believers' support.

Embracing the Sync of Unity

In a world of connection, unity stands as a potent shield. God's network is strong and has many devices (believers) synced to the network. This spiritual community helps to reinforce our security. Just as synchronized devices strengthen a network, the harmony of our spiritual community reinforces our security. Acts 2:42–47 testify to this unity's power, showcasing how a collective of believers can be a formidable defense.

Empowered for Sync Success

Let this truth resonate: Spiritual attacks do not define our divine sync; instead, they refine it. Challenges serve as sculptors, shaping our discernment, faith, and resilience. Our journey is not solitary; it's a dynamic partnership with the Lord. By embracing this principle, we're protecting and fortifying our connection.

The Path Forward

Take some time and meditate on this chapter. Consider the barriers that might interrupt your seamless connection with

the Lord. Engage in prayerful reflection to identify distractions, doubts, or the chaos of busyness that may disrupt your spiritual reception. Commit to cultivating spiritual sensitivity through regular prayer and immersion in God's Word. Embrace spiritual disciplines and seek the Lord's guidance to navigate your challenges. Persevere with faith as you overcome obstacles and actively guard against spiritual assaults.

You troubleshoot and optimize your connections in the realm of digital technology. Your commitment to addressing barriers in divine sync enhances your uninterrupted spiritual connection with the Lord. Remember, challenges may shake you, but your bond with the Lord remains unbreakable.

Chapter 9

Bandwidth Expansion: Expanding Your Capacity for Divine Connection

The world of technology has gifted us the marvel of data transfer through expanded bandwidth. The smooth flow of information enhances our experience. Our devices work better with higher bandwidth. Faster downloads and smoother streaming are all possible because of an expanded capacity to handle more significant amounts of data. Now, think of your spiritual life in the same way. Just as an expanded bandwidth allows for improved data transfer, you have the potential to expand your spiritual capacity for a deeper and more meaningful connection with The Lord.

Recognizing the Need for Expansion

On your journey with God, have you felt a longing for more? A yearning for deeper intimacy, broader understanding, and a wider impact in His kingdom? It's essential to recognize this need for expansion.

When we desire to go deeper with God, we open ourselves to transformation and growth that can significantly impact our spiritual journey.

Think of expansion as stepping into a larger room. The more spacious the room, the more we can bring in, experience, and enjoy. Expanding our spiritual capacity works similarly; it creates a larger space within us for God to fill. This larger space, in turn, allows for a richer connection and an increased ability to receive His guidance and revelation. We can handle deeper insights, richer experiences, and a profound connection with the Lord through a spiritually expanded capacity.

Spiritual Growth Equals Expansion

Expanding our capacity for connection with the Lord begins with a commitment to spiritual growth. Sometimes, this expansion requires a change, much like transferring contents from one bowl to a larger one. As we grow spiritually, our minds and hearts become like those larger bowls, able to hold more of God's wisdom, love, and revelation.

Renewing our minds is crucial to this process. Romans 12:2 reminds us not to conform to the patterns of this world but to be transformed by renewing our minds. Consider how renewing our mind through studying The Scriptures, meditating on God's Word, and embracing a positive perspective can expand our capacity for understanding and connection.

Embracing a Larger Perspective

Do you sometimes find your connection with God limited by your understanding? Embracing a larger perspective of God and His kingdom can open new relationship dimensions. Just as a bigger window provides a broader view, expanding your perspective allows you to see more of God's love, purposes, and ways.

We should take time to learn from the spiritual experiences of others and develop a global outlook by exploring diverse perspectives. Doing so increases our potential to grasp God's work from various perspectives, fostering a closer relationship with Him.

Seeking Deeper Levels of Intimacy

The beauty of deepening our connection with The Lord is that it brings deeper intimacy with Him. Think of a close friendship: the more time invested in that relationship, the more intimate the relationship becomes. The same applies to our relationship with God.

Imagine the intimate relationship between Moses and God. Exodus 33:11 mentions that God spoke to Moses face-to-face, as a man speaks with his friend. Moses cultivated a level of intimacy that expanded his capacity to connect with God in remarkable ways. Pursue this level of intimacy by dedicating time to prayer, practicing worship as a lifestyle, and surrendering fully to God.

Identifying Obstacles: Clearing the Pathway

As with any journey, obstacles can arise. In our pursuit of divine sync, it's crucial to identify and understand the spiritual barriers that may hinder our bandwidth expansion. Sometimes, spiritual expansion is not limited by doubt or fear. Instead, it's limited by the prioritization of The Lord in our lives. Recall Martha and Mary—their differing approaches teach us the value of prioritizing The Lord's presence amidst life's demands. Further, imagine if the Israelites had succumbed to their ignorance when facing the Red Sea. Their lack of knowledge of God and His power could have caused them to miss the miraculous parting of the waters.

I must say this to you - keeping God as a priority will keep the pathway clear and allow spiritual expansion. Realize the truth in God's Word, immerse yourself in His promises, and embrace your identity as His beloved child. Continue to seek Him first and His righteousness. You can genuinely expand your capacity for connection and embrace the fullness of what God has for you.

Perseverance and Faith: Troubleshooting Challenges

An expanded bandwidth will require continuous troubleshooting. This action requires faith and perseverance. As our device (spirit) maintains connection amidst disruptions, our faithfulness must persist through challenges. When fiery darts of life are flying, or doubt rears its ugly head, we must remain faithful to The Lord.

Practices to Expand Spiritual Bandwidth

- **Prayer and Meditation**: Just as we expand our internet bandwidth, we can expand our spiritual capacity through consistent prayer and meditation. These practices create space for God's wisdom to flow freely into our lives.

- **Scripture Study**: Delving deeper into the Word of God enhances our understanding and equips us to handle more profound spiritual insights.

- **Fasting**: Just as clearing cache improves internet speed, fasting clears spiritual clutter, allowing for a more unobstructed flow of divine downloads.

- **Community Engagement**: Engaging with a community of believers provides diverse perspectives, enriching our spiritual bandwidth.

- **Service**: Serving others opens our hearts to new experiences and insights, expanding our capacity to receive from God.

As technology advances with expanded bandwidth, allowing for smoother data transfer and enhanced experiences, our spiritual life can also expand. As a call for expansion, consider the longing for deeper intimacy, a broader understanding, and a wider impact in God's kingdom. This journey involves renewing your mind, embracing a larger perspective of God's kingdom, and seeking deeper levels of intimacy with Him.

Our spiritual capacity expands as we identify obstacles, clear them, and troubleshoot challenges with perseverance and faith. We must keep God as our priority, immerse ourselves in His Word, and continue seeking Him. As our spiritual bandwidth grows and our relationship with God deepens, embrace His fullness.

Chapter 10

Beyond Wi-Fi:
The Eternal Connection

As we embark on this chapter of this extraordinary journey, let's explore the realm beyond Wi-Fi's limitations and earthly networks. Imagine a connection with God that transcends time and distance constraints, much like the wireless bonds enabled by modern technology. In this chapter, we'll explore the unbreakable bond we share with our Creator, one that defies the boundaries of this world.

Uninterrupted Sync:
Enjoying Eternal Communion with God

Consider the joy of an uninterrupted sync with God—a profound and enduring communion that nothing can sever. Just as Bluetooth devices remain connected through distractions and disruptions, we can maintain an unbroken connection with God's presence in every circumstance. In moments of joy and challenges, we find solace, strength, and guidance in His constant company. Psalm 16:11 assures us,

"Thou wilt shew me the path of life: in thy presence is fullness of joy; at thy right hand, there are pleasures forevermore." Think of the example set by Jesus, who remained intimately connected with the Father through prayer and communion even in the busiest and most trying times of His ministry.

Let's draw inspiration from biblical figures whose lives mirror this eternal bond. Think of Enoch, who walked so closely with God that he was taken into His presence without experiencing death (Genesis 5:24). Reflect on the words of the Apostle Paul in Philippians 3:10–11, where he expresses his deep longing to know Christ and be found in Him. These examples emphasize that our connection with God extends beyond our earthly existence.

Infinite Storage:

Exploring the Limitless Depths of God's Wisdom and Revelation

Much like cloud storage that accommodates endless data, we are invited to explore the limitless depths of God's wisdom and revelation. We dig into passages like Ephesians 3:20, which reminds us that God can do far more abundantly beyond what we ask or imagine. Our pursuit leads us to tap into His infinite wisdom, knowledge, and understanding reserves. As we dive into Ephesians 3:16–19, we find Paul's prayer for the Ephesian believers to grasp the vastness of God's love and glory. James 1:5 urges us to seek wisdom from above, with the promise that God generously imparts it.

But remember, this everlasting connection isn't just about sharing information. It's about building a deep relationship with our Creator, an opportunity to explore the limitless treasures of His Kingdom.

As we embrace this eternal connection, we discover the joy of unbroken fellowship with God, bask in the fullness of His presence, and experience the delight of eternal communion. Christ's words in John 15:5 resonate: "I am the vine, ye are the branches: He that abideth in me, and I in him, the same bringeth forth much fruit: for without me ye can do nothing." This eternal connection empowers us to live out our purpose, drawing on divine wisdom and walking confidently in our identity as His beloved children.

Let's stand at the doorway of our forever connection with God. Let's commit to growing closer to Him, knowing He eagerly desires our company and wants to show us the amazing things in His kingdom. Let the stories of those who trusted in this connection inspire us. And may we live each day with confidence in our unbreakable bond with God, both in this life and forevermore.

Beyond the limits of earthly connections, beyond Bluetooth and Wi-Fi, there's an eternal bond—an invitation to discover God's deep love, wisdom, and presence. Embrace this truth; let it reshape your life and lead your way. This eternal connection offers fulfillment, purpose, and joy that surpasses

anything in this world. As you move forward, may you walk in the glow of this relationship, with God's grace, love, and purpose guiding every step of your journey.

Closing Thoughts

Living a Life in Sync with God

In these closing thoughts, I want us to reflect on the incredible journey we have embarked upon throughout "Divine Sync" and embrace the destiny that awaits us. We have explored the power of divine connection and learned to navigate the complexities of syncing with God's purposes.

We recognize that our lives are not random but purposefully designed by our Creator. Every moment, every decision, and every relationship have a role in God's redemptive plan. We, as believers, live in harmony with His divine design, allowing our lives to align with His purposes and contribute to the beauty of His masterpiece.

As we reflect on the key lessons we have learned, we understand that syncing to the divine network is not a one-time event but a lifelong pursuit. It requires constant surrender, a posture of humility, and a deep yearning for intimacy with God. Just as we ensure our devices stay connected to Wi-Fi for seamless access to information and communication, we must stay connected to God for continuous spiritual guidance and growth. We have seen how to discern the presence of the Lord, receive divine downloads, and navigate the complexities of our world. We have witnessed the transformation that occurs when we yield to the work of the Holy Spirit and embrace the updates and upgrades God has for us.

Let us commit to living a life in sync with God's plan. Let us walk in obedience, following His lead with unwavering faith. Let us cultivate a heart of gratitude and worship, acknowledging His goodness and faithfulness in every season. Let us continually seek His wisdom, allowing His Word to guide our steps and shape our perspectives. Just as we routinely check and reconnect our devices to Wi-Fi, let us make it a priority to reconnect with God daily through prayer, worship, and study of His Word. And let us boldly step into the fullness of our divine calling, knowing that we are an essential part of His work in the world.

As we approach the conclusion of this journey, consider the following question:

How can I maintain and deepen my connection with God daily, ensuring that my life remains in sync with His divine purposes?

Here are a few suggestions:

1. Embrace Time with the Lord:

    -   Imagine starting each day with a warm conversation with God and diving into the rich, life-giving waters of the Bible. Let your heart overflow with praise and gratitude. Feel the connection grow as you pour out your heart, share your dreams, and seek His guidance. Let prayer be your lifeline, keeping you in love with His love and wisdom.

2. Live in Obedience:

    -   Feel the excitement of stepping out in faith, knowing you are following God's perfect plan for your life. Listen for His voice; when He calls, respond with a resounding "Yes, Lord!" Experience the joy of walking in His ways and seeing His purposes unfold in your life.

3. Practice Spiritual Disciplines:

    -   Discover the power of fasting and meditation. Let these practices draw you closer to God, stripping away distractions and focusing your heart on Him. Feel the deep connection from these intentional times of seeking His presence.

4. Reflect and Reevaluate:

   • Take moments to reflect on your spiritual journey with God. Celebrate how far you've come and dream about where God is leading you next. Where you are now is not your final destination. The Lord has more in store for you.

5. Welcome to the Holy Spirit:

   • Open your heart wide to the Holy Spirit's guidance. Feel His presence transform you from the inside out, filling you with His power and grace. Let the frequency of His voice be the sound that guides your steps, bringing you closer to God's heart each day.

May the lessons learned in "Divine Sync: Maintaining a Strong Spiritual Connection with God" continue to resonate in your hearts and minds. Someone needs you today, and you must remain in daily touch with the Lord to ensure your life is in sync with His plans.

As this book comes to a close, remember that your journey is just beginning. Just as you diligently maintain your digital connections for efficiency and productivity, nurture your spiritual connections for a life of purpose, fulfillment, and eternal impact. Let the principles and insights you've discovered ignite a lifelong pursuit of divine connection. Sync to the divine network every day and let your life shine with the glory of God.

As you follow the leading of the Holy Spirit, revisit this book. If you want to rekindle or deepen your relationship with God, return to these pages. Keep yourself tuned in and synchronized with Him, allowing His wisdom and guidance to mold your life constantly. Remember this: Work the Word and the Word will Work for You!

"I am the vine, ye are the branches: He that abideth in me, and I in him, the same bringeth forth much fruit: for without me ye can do nothing." John 15:5 (KJV)

Stay Connected

A Prayer to Strengthen Your Divine Connection

Father God, as I come to You today...

I've just finished this book, and reflecting on the journey I have undertaken, I come before You with a heart full of gratitude. Thank You for the revelations, wisdom, and guidance You have poured into my life through these pages.

Lord, I desire to sync my heart and life with Yours, aligning myself fully with Your divine will. Just as I maintain my digital connections for efficiency, please help me to nurture my spiritual connection with You diligently. May I stay attuned to Your voice, ready to receive Your divine downloads and walk in Your wisdom.

Father, expand my capacity to connect with You. Let my mind and heart be like vessels, open and ready to be filled with more of Your love, grace, and understanding. Help me to embrace spiritual growth, transferring my thoughts and desires into Your hands and allowing Your plans to unfold in my life.

Holy Spirit, guide me as I commit to daily prayer, worship, and the study of Your Word. Just as I rely on Wi-Fi to stay connected, let me rely on Your presence to navigate every moment of my life. Clear away any distractions or clutter that hinder my connection with You. Protect me with Your spiritual firewall, guarding my heart and mind from negative influences.

Lord, I seek Your divine alignment. Help me to live in obedience, following Your lead with unwavering faith. Fill me with a heart of gratitude and worship, acknowledging Your goodness in every season. As I serve others, let Your love and grace flow through me, empowering me to make a positive impact.

Father, I embrace the automatic updates You bring into my life, transforming me day by day into Your image. May I continuously grow in my understanding of Your ways, remaining open to the work of the Holy Spirit.

As I step into this new chapter, I ask for Your strength and courage to pursue a lifelong connection with You. May the lessons I have learned resonate in my heart and mind, propelling me toward a deeper, more vibrant relationship with You.

Thank You, Lord, for the journey of Divine Sync. Let me walk in Your purpose, plan, and will for my life, bringing You glory every step of the way and staying continually connected with You.

In Jesus' name, I pray,

Amen.

Connection Keys

Sync Glossary of Terms

Automatic Updates:

- Updates automatically applied to software without user intervention ensure the system remains current and secure. This statement in the book symbolizes the ongoing spiritual growth and continuous improvement of one's faith and connection with God, which occurs automatically when we're in sync with Him.

Bandwidth:

- The maximum rate of data transfer across a given path. It's used in the book to describe the capacity to receive and process spiritual insights and revelations.

Cache:

- A smaller, faster memory component that stores copies of frequently accessed data for quick retrieval. It's used in the book to refer to the need to clear mental clutter to better receive divine insights.

Cloud:

- Internet-based computing that provides shared processing resources and data to computers and other devices on demand. In the book, it is used to describe a higher spiritual realm where divine insights and guidance are stored and accessed.

Divine Sync:

- The process of aligning oneself spiritually with God, ensuring continuous connection and communication with Him.

Downloads:

- The act of receiving data from a remote system, typically from the internet, to a local device. It's used in the book to refer to Divine Downloads, which are insights, wisdom, and revelations received directly from God, often during prayer or meditation.

Fasting:

- Abstaining from food or certain activities for a period of time to focus on spiritual growth and seek God's guidance.

Intercessory Prayer:

- A form of prayer where an individual prays on behalf of others, seeking God's intervention and blessings for them.

Network:

- A group of interconnected devices that share resources and information. In the book, it refers to the community of believers and the connection to God's divine plan.

Prophetic Anointing:

- A spiritual empowerment God gives to a person, enabling them to speak God's messages with authority and clarity.

Real-Time Information:

- Data that is delivered immediately after collection without delay. Used in the book to describe the immediate and direct guidance received from God.

Revelation:

- Knowledge or insight revealed by God, often providing direction, correction, or encouragement.

Spiritual Disciplines:

- Practices such as prayer, fasting, Bible study, and meditation that help individuals grow in their faith and spiritual connection with God.

Spiritual Firewall:

- In the natural, a firewall is a security system that protects against unauthorized access or threats in a computer network. Metaphorically, it is used in the book to describe protecting one's spiritual life from negative influences and attacks.

Spiritual Growth:

- The process of developing a deeper relationship with God and maturing in one's faith and character.

The Holy Spirit:

- In Christian belief, the third person of the Trinity, who guides, empowers, and comforts believers.

Syncing (Synchronization):

- The process of making sure that data or information is consistent and up-to-date across multiple devices or platforms. In the context of the book, it refers to aligning one's spiritual life with God's will.

Wi-Fi:

- A technology that allows electronic devices to connect to the internet wirelessly within a certain area. Used metaphorically in the book to describe a seamless, continuous connection with God.

Worship:

- Acts of devotion and praise directed towards God, often involving singing, prayer, and reflection.

About the Author

Dr. Tonya Williams

Dr. Tonya Williams is the founder and pastor of the multi-faceted Dr. Tonya Williams Ministries and the pastor of Releasing Living Waters Ministries. Her accurate and authentic prophetic anointing often calls for her to deliver life-changing words to God's people through conferences, workshops, retreats, and seminars. Her commitment to spiritual growth and her ability to translate complex spiritual concepts into practical, everyday wisdom make her a sought-after speaker and mentor.

Dr. Williams is the CEO and Founder of Visionaries, Women on the Move, Inc., a non-profit women's organization that develops support initiatives to empower women to attain their goals and achieve success.

Additionally, Dr. Williams hosts the monthly talk show, where, through The Holy Spirit, she empowers God's people to rise above their current circumstances and pursue God's plans for their lives. Her inspirational and uplifting messages are delivered through coaching and mentoring experiences, enabling individuals to live up to their highest dreams. She has established mentoring programs for women called The Fabulous 10 and Being Authentically You.

Every year, Dr. Williams organizes the Intercessory Prayer Summit, a powerful prayer conference that propels many individuals into their next level of prayer. She also conducts

a weekly prayer call for intercessory prayer, known as the Aroma of Prayer. She delivers weekly sermons on her platforms, Power Gathering, and her podcast, Embracing Pivotal Moments.

Dr. Williams holds a degree in theology and leadership and has been actively involved in her church community, leading Bible studies, prayer groups, and spiritual retreats. Her profound experiences and divine revelations are the foundation for her writing and ministry.

Through her book, "Divine Sync," Dr. Williams aims to share the transformative power of staying connected to God's divine network, encouraging readers to align their lives with His purposes and experience the fullness of His love and guidance.

Made in the USA
Columbia, SC
05 January 2025

51159631R00046